**Strive for Peace
With all your Heart**

PSALM 34 v 14

𝒯o . . . .

ℱrom . . . .

It is a great thing, this reading of the Scriptures! For it is not possible ever to exhaust the mind of the scriptures. It is a well that has no bottom.

JOHN CHRYSOSTOM

SPECIAL PAGES

INCLUDING SELECTIONS FROM THE GOOD NEWS BIBLE

THOUGHTS, PRAYERS, PRAISE AND HELPLINES

A helping hand again and again

**Compiled and Published by
GORDON EARL
under the imprint of GRE Publisher
BUCKHURST HILL
ESSEX**

SCRIPTURES QUOTED FROM THE GOOD NEWS BIBLE PUBLISHED BY THE BIBLE SOCIETIES/HARPER COLLINS PUBLISHING LTD UK. USED WITH PERMISSION.
© AMERICAN BIBLE SOCIETY, 1966, 1971, 1976, 1992

All rights reserved.
No part of this publication may be reproduced or transmitted, in any form or by any means, electronic or mechanical, including photography, recording or any information storage and retrieval system, without permission in writing from the publisher and also, where applicable, the copyright holders.

First lines of hymns/songs courtesy of Marshall Pickering, an imprint of Harper Collins Publishers. Any other copyright omission regretted with apologies.

Printed 1995

ISBN 0 9525507 0 9

Typesetting by Freedom Design, London E4 9PS - Telephone 0181 531 1844
Typefaces throughout: ITC Quorum, Cascade Script

Printed in Great Britain for
GRE PUBLISHER
The St. John's Church Centre, High Road, Buckhurst Hill, Essex, IG9 5RX
by The Bath Press (Division of BPMG)
Lower Bristol Road, BA2 3BL - Telephone 01225 428101
London Office: Bloomsbury House, 23 Bedford Square, London WC1B 3HH - Telephone 0171 637 9700

Illustrations courtesy of Slim Wilkinson, Tunbridge Wells - Telephone 0892 534185

CONTENTS

Our reading of the Gospel story can and should be an act of personal communion with the Living Lord

WILLIAM TEMPLE

CONTENTS

10	HISTORY LEADING TO THE LORD'S PRAYER	
11	THE LORD'S PRAYER	
12	HISTORY LEADING TO THE TEN COMMANDMENTS	
13	THE TEN COMMANDMENTS	
15	ANGER	Isle of Man
16	ASSURANCE	
17	ATTITUDE	Kent & Sussex
18	AUTHORITY	
19	BAD NEWS	Scotland
20	BEHAVIOUR	
21	BODY	Somerset
22	DEATH	
23	DECISIONS	Midlands
24	DIRECTION	
25	DISCIPLINE	Lancashire
26	DOUBT	
27	ENVY	Gwynedd
28	FAITH	
29	FAMILY	Dorset
30	FEAR	
31	FORGIVENESS	Northumberland
32	FRIENDSHIP	
33	FRUSTRATION	Hampshire
34	GOD'S DAY	
35	GOD'S PURPOSE	Norfolk
36	GUILT	

37	HEAVEN	Isle of Wight
38	HELL	
39	HONESTY	Cumbria
40	JOY	
41	LAW	Northern Ireland
42	LONELINESS	
43	LOVE	Essex
44	NEEDS	
45	PATIENCE	Yorkshire
46	PEACE	
47	PRAISE	London
48	PRAYER	
49	PROBLEMS	Wales
50	RICHES	
51	SEX	Wiltshire
52	SHARING	
53	SIN	Cornwall
54	SORROW	
55	SUFFERING	Cambridgeshire
56	TALENTS	
57	TEMPTATION	Derbyshire
58	TIME	
59	TRUTH	Cornwall
60	WISDOM	
61	WORK	Somerset
62 ☎	HELPLINES	

Illustrations separate to page content.

Dedicated to my four children - Simon who returned to God - never forgotten and Paul, Helen and Joanne, who's support and love I treasure; also to all my family and all my friends everywhere.

Those who know you, Lord, will trust you.

PSALM 9 v 10

FOREWORD

'How I came to compile these pages" and "Turning to advantage a previous disadvantage" are just two of the alternative headings which have come to mind as I researched extensively how these pages could be brought together. However, ducking the true issue is not allowed and FOLLOWING THE WILL OF GOD actually hits the nail on the head - the next few lines will explain further. First, it is hoped that no matter where you, the reader, are positioned in your own lifetime journey, there may be genuine help and improved well-being as you read these pages. Secondly that you will know of someone else - a friend or relative, maybe a teenager - who could also benefit by being given a copy of this booklet for themselves as a BIRTHDAY GIFT, CONFIRMATION CELEBRATION, at a DIFFICULT or SAD TIME, at a CROSSROADS or when BEREAVEMENT is at hand. Our duty is to help one another.

What makes a Christian? Is it being brought up in a Christian home? Or because one's parents go to church? Not so. Is it because one constantly helps other people? Or because of infant Baptism or the act of Confirmation? Not so, but nearly there. Being a Christian is when a person recognises and believes that Jesus is the Son of God, did walk on this earth just as we do and did die faultlessly a horrible death on the cross, and that this did happen as a plan to save mankind from their inherited sinful nature. Being a Christian is when that person asks the risen Lord into their own life and repents sincerely of the wrong doings that have already happened, with every good intention of not allowing deliberate sin to happen again. SIMPLE - YET AMAZINGLY CHALLENGING. It needs a lot of thought, encouragement AND PRAYER. Humbly, this is the testimony of where I, together with thousands of others, stand before our Creator and Saviour.

Towards the end of this book are HELPLINES where the reader can request further TOTALLY CONFIDENTIAL information - a free service for all who care to ask.

Gordon Earl
Spring 1995

The background leading to the first using of the Lord's Prayer

Whilst the first four books in the New Testament, the four Gospels, give to all following generations including ourselves, an account of much of the travelling and ministering of Jesus Christ, it is interesting to note that initially all the teachings were memory-retained by his closest followers, and not actually committed in written form until a considerable number of years after the death of Jesus. Also that although recorded by different writers, at separate times and in different places, many of those precious biblical recollections which we are now able to read today, are almost identical - word for word - by the different writers. It is recorded in Scripture that the disciple scribes would be given a special clarity of memory for this purpose.

The words universally known as the LORD'S PRAYER, were spoken by none other than Jesus himself, whilst here on earth and to his closest followers - his disciples, in direct reply to their request to Jesus as to how to pray. The LORD'S PRAYER surely represents the most well known, most widely used, most prayed words, by countless hundreds of thousands of Christians each and every day the whole world over.

Sometimes because of the frequency of use, the full depth of meaning can inadvertently be skimmed over and it is to be highly recommended to yourself, the reader, no matter who or where you are at this time, that you reread at less than one half the normal speed of reading, these wonderful God-given words, thereby soaking into your very being, the true depth, meaning and purpose. Truly a . . .

PRAYER ABOVE ALL OTHER PRAYERS

THE LORD'S PRAYER

Jesus commanded his disciples saying . . "when you pray, do not use a lot of meaningless words . . .Your Father (God) already knows what you need before you ask him.

This is then how you should pray . . .

>Our Father in heaven,
>hallowed be your name,
>your kingdom come,
>your will be done,
>on earth as in heaven.
>Give us today our daily bread.
>Forgive us our sins
>as we forgive those who sin against us.
>Lead us not into temptation
>but deliver us from evil.
>
>For the kingdom, the power, and the glory are yours
>now and for ever.

Amen

THE TEN COMMANDMENTS
Historically placed

These few words from a most profound story (as taken from the second book in the Holy Bible - the book of EXODUS) are of the Life of Moses, chosen by God to be the leader of all the Israelite people. We read that the Pharaoh of Egypt at that time was demanding all Israelite sons be killed because in his opinion the Israelite people were becoming too numerous. We read on of the baby Israelite Moses being hidden in the bulrushes, that he might not be put to death, and of being found by none other than Pharaoh's own daughter, who then chose to bring him up as her own child. Although Moses was brought up as an Egyptian, he never forgot he was an Israelite by birth, and as an adult heard and responded to the call of God, that he should become the leader of his people.

We read of the burning bush and of God talking directly to Moses and preparing him for what lay ahead. His brother Aaron should be beside him as his spokesman. Moses spoke to Pharaoh on behalf of the Israelites and because Pharaoh was not prepared to listen, there then followed a series of ten catastrophic plagues over the land of Egypt. Pharaoh eventually allowed Moses to lead his people away from slavery and they travelled towards the Red Sea.

Scripture further recounts the parting of the waters giving the Israelites a safe passage, the waters then capturing and drowning the pursuing Egyptians. Moses now led his people into the Sinai desert, and after much wandering, with further stories of the miraculous provision of food - Manna (a plant substance) and water, they did then settle at the foot of Mount Sinai. God commanded Moses to go alone onto the mountain to pray for three days, and it was recorded that on the third day, with much thunder, lightning and earth shakings, the voice of God came loudly to Moses and God spoke with Moses and gave to him two flat tablets of stone, upon which were marked the TEN COMMANDMENTS.

THE TEN COMMANDMENTS

"I am the Lord your God, and these are my commandments, to be obeyed by all my people.

You shall worship no other God than me.
You shall not make any statue or picture to worship.
You shall not speak the name of the Lord,
except with reverence.
You shall keep the Sabbath, the seventh day, as a
holy day of rest, for in six days I made the world,
and on the seventh day I rested.
You shall show respect for your father
and your mother.
You shall not commit murder.
You shall not be unfaithful to your wife.
You shall not steal.
You shall not speak falsely against others.
You shall not envy the possessions
of another person."

When the people heard the thunder and saw the flames and the smoke, they were afraid and would not come near. Moses reassured them. "Do not fear", he said. "God has come to us so that we might learn His Commandments and keep ourselves free from sin".

There is then the continuing story in the book of Exodus of how the many disbelievers soon lost their lives, but those who believed were lead by Moses out of darkness and "into the promised land".

FURTHER READINGS

Matthew Ch 22 v 37-40	Jesus reminding the local Pharisees of obedience to the Commandments.
Matthew Ch 19 v 18-24	Jesus explaining to a rich young man the only way to Heaven through obedience to the Commandments.

ANGER

EPHESIANS Ch 4 v 26
If you become angry, do not let your anger lead you into sin and do not stay angry all day v 27.. Don't give the devil a chance.

COLOSSIANS Ch 3 v 8
But now you must get rid of all these things; anger, passion and hateful feelings. No insults or obscene talk must ever come from your lips.

PROVERBS Ch 19 v 11
If you are sensible you will control your temper. When someone wrongs you, it is a virtue to ignore it.

PSALM 103 v 8
The Lord is merciful and loving, slow to become angry and full of constant love.

PROVERBS Ch 15 v 1
A gentle answer quietens anger, but a harsh one stirs it up.

FURTHER READINGS

Romans Ch 1 v 18   1 Corinthians Ch 4 v 5   Luke Ch 6 v 27-28
James Ch 3 v 8-10

THOUGHT
Anger sometimes stems from our own short tempers, sometimes through justifiable circumstances. A caution because (a proverb)...He who angers you, conquers you.

PRAYER
Lord help me to see a way through this current disappointment/annoyance, a way towards calmer times again. No matter where the fault may be Lord, give me the grace to forgive, to forget and to foster a new way forward.

SO LET IT BE.

Rushen Castle - Isle of Man

♫ CHRIST IS THE ANSWER ♫

ASSURANCE

HEBREWS Ch 13 v 5
For God has said, "I will never leave you. I will never abandon you"

JAMES Ch 1 v 17
Every good gift and every perfect present comes from heaven. It comes down from God, the creator of the heavenly lights, who does not change or cause darkness by turning.

JOHN Ch 14 v 27
Peace is what I leave with you; it is my own peace that I give you.

PHILIPPIANS Ch 4 v 7
And God's peace, which is far beyond human understanding, will keep your hearts and minds safe in union with Christ Jesus.

FURTHER READINGS

Psalm 19 v 7   Lamentations Ch 5 v 19   1 Peter Ch 3 v 10-12
Isaiah Ch 4 v 1-20

THOUGHT

So often lifetime difficulties beset us: loneliness, insufficient money, housing difficulties, challenges at school or at the workplace. Assurance we need and assurance we need to give.

PRAYER

Lord God you know the individual needs of each and every one of us, Graciously uphold us with your unfailing assurance through these uncertain times, and guide us into the way forward again.

SO LET IT BE

♪ **BLESSED ASSURANCE JESUS IS MINE** ♫

17

ATTITUDE

ROMANS Ch 12 v 9-11
Love must be completely sincere. Hate what is evil, hold on to what is good. Love one another warmly as Christian brothers and be eager to show respect for one another. Work hard and do not be lazy. Serve the Lord with a heart full of devotion.

1 CORINTHIANS Ch 16 v 13-14
Be alert, stand firm in the faith, be brave, be strong. Do all your work in love.

PROVERBS Ch 16 v 18-19
Pride leads to destruction and arrogance to downfall. It is better to be humble and stay poor than to be one of the arrogant.

PROVERBS Ch 17 v 22
Being cheerful keeps you healthy. It is a slow death to be gloomy all the time.

FURTHER READINGS

1 Thessalonians Ch 5 v 18	2 Timothy Ch 2 v 25-26	Hebrews Ch 13 v 17
1 Peter Ch 4 v 8 &14	1 John Ch 2 v 9	Proverbs Ch 17 v 22

THOUGHT

Your own soul is nourished when you are kind towards others. It is destroyed when a person is cruel.

PRAYER

Help me Lord to understand that with the right attitude I can achieve so much more for the good of this world. That every time I help another person in whatever instance is presented to me, large or small, that this will be good in Your sight.

SO LET IT BE.

Oast houses in Kent and Sussex

♪ **ALL HAIL THE POWER OF JESUS NAME** ♪

AUTHORITY

ROMANS Ch 13 v 1
Everyone must obey the state authorities, because no authority exists without God's permission, and the existing authorities have been put there by God.

EPHESIANS Ch 6 v 1
Children, it is your Christian duty to obey your parents, for this is the right thing to do.

LUKE Ch 12 v 5
... fear God, who ... has the authority to throw you into hell. Believe me, he is the one you must fear.

PSALM 102 v 12
But you, O Lord, are King for ever: all generations will remember you.

FURTHER READINGS

Matthew Ch 22 v 21-40   Job Ch 36 v 10-12   Matthew Ch 7 v 29
Mark Ch 1 v 27

THOUGHT

Just how would our busy inner cities cope without traffic lights? Just how would children grow and mature without guiding parents and authoritative school teachers?

PRAYER

Lord God, without guidance and direction within our Lives we would soon be hopelessly lost! Give to us an understanding of your almighty authority and an obedience to hear and follow that which you have planned for the good of each one of us, and especially for myself at this time.

SO LET IT BE

♪ **I HAVE DECIDED TO FOLLOW JESUS** ♪

BAD NEWS

ISAIAH Ch 40 v 28-31
Don't you know? Haven't you heard? The Lord is the everlasting God; he created all the world. He never grows tired or weary. . . . He strengthens.

1 PETER Ch 5 v 7
Leave all your worries with God, because he cares for you.

PSALM 46 v 1
God is our shelter and strength, always ready to help in times of trouble.

HEBREWS Ch 4 v 13
There is nothing that can be hidden from God; everything in all creation is exposed and lies open before his eyes.

FURTHER READINGS

Psalm 59 v 9   *Matthew Ch 7 v 7-8*   *Romans Ch 12 v 15*
Psalm 147 v 3

THOUGHT

After the essential rainfall comes the warming sunshine. After the loss of a loved one or a time of severe testing, comes a period of readjustment and hope for the future. Just as always the day follows the night.

PRAYER

Heavenly Father, you have given to us a short but plentiful Life. You have ordained both GOOD and BAD in your almighty plan. Help us to accept with grace and understanding, the upsets and the bad news which we do suffer, and give us a faith to see that new beginnings will soon be with us.

SO LET IT BE

The Scottish Highlands

♪ **FATHER HEAR THE PRAYER WE OFFER** ♫

BEHAVIOUR

2 CORINTHIANS Ch 6 v 4
In everything we do, we show that we are God's servants by patiently enduring troubles, hardships and difficulties.

EPHESIANS Ch 5 v 15-16
So be careful how you live. Don't live like ignorant people, but like wise people. Make good use of every opportunity you have.

GALATIANS Ch 6 v 4-5
Each one should judge his own conduct. If it is good, then he can be proud of what he has done, without having to compare it with what someone else has done. For everyone has to carry his own load.

PHILIPPIANS Ch 2 v 3-4
Don't do anything from selfish ambition or from a cheap desire to boast, . . . always considering others better than yourselves.

FURTHER READINGS

Colossians Ch 3 v 5-10   *1 Timothy Ch 1 v 19*   *James Ch 3 v 8-9*
1 Peter Ch 1 v 13-15   *Proverbs Ch 10 v 14*   *Proverbs Ch 15 v 1*
1 John Ch 3 v 18

THOUGHT

We learn from our parents, yet from time to time we rebel. The good behaviour of those older than us is sometimes irksome and we let the side down. Quite simply we slip up. Good behaviour costs nothing yet gives much.

PRAYER

It is amazing, almost beyond our understanding, how you O God, are able to see every single move that everyone of us makes, no matter that there are so many millions of us! Help us to guard our behaviour at all times in a way befitting your guardianship over us.

SO LET IT BE.

♪ **SEEK YE FIRST THE KINGDOM OF GOD** ♪

BODY

PROVERBS Ch 17 v 22
Being cheerful keeps you healthy. It is slow death to be gloomy all the time.

ROMANS Ch 12 v 1
So then, my brothers, because of God's great mercy to us I appeal to you, offer yourselves as a living sacrifice to God, dedicated to his service and pleasing to him.

1 CORINTHIANS Ch 6 v 19
Don't you know that your body is the temple of the Holy Spirit, who lives in you and who was given to you by God.

JOB Ch 14 v 1-2
We are all born weak and helpless. We lead the same short, troubled life. We grow and wither as quickly as flowers; we disappear like shadows.

FURTHER READINGS

1 Corinthians Ch 9 v 27   *Proverbs Ch 15 v 13*   *Hebrews Ch 4 v 1*
                              Proverbs Ch 18 v 14

THOUGHT

So easy to take for granted, the precision of our arms and legs, of sight and hearing. Central to our movement is the heart, central to our thinking is the brain - incredible constructions indeed.

PRAYER

God Almighty, you have chosen to create the human body, so intricately and in your own image. Keep us ever mindful of this wondrous gift, keep us fit and well and help us through times of hurt and incapacity.

SO LET IT BE.

Burrington rock, Somerset

♪ **JESUS TAKE ME AS I AM** ♪

DEATH

JOHN Ch 11 v 25-26
Jesus said . . ."I am the resurrection and the life. Whoever believes in me will live, even though he dies; and whoever lives and believes in me will never die. Do you believe this?"

REVELATION Ch 21 v 3-4
. . . "Now God's home is with mankind! He will live with them, and they shall be his people. . . . He will wipe away all tears from their eyes. There will be no more death, no more grief or crying or pain. The old things have disappeared.

2 CORINTHIANS Ch 5 v 1
For we know that when the tent we live in - our body here on earth - is torn down, God will have a house in heaven for us to live in, a home he himself has made, and which will last forever.

JONAH Ch 2 v 7
When I felt my life slipping away, then O Lord, I prayed to you, and in your holy temple you heard me.

FURTHER READINGS

1 Corinthians Ch 15 v 22   Psalm 23 v 4   John Ch 14 v 1-4
Hebrews Ch 9 v 27

THOUGHT

Never were we to be given an earthly life forever. We have long known of normal life expectancy and of unexpected shortenings through tragedy or illness. Our life, a gift from God, and eventually back into the presence of God.

PRAYER

Help us Lord God, to understand that Death, whilst so painful to those left behind, should also be looked upon as the gateway to eternal life with you. Give us an acceptance of your redemption through the sacrifice of your son Jesus Christ.

SO LET IT BE.

♪ **THE DAY THOU GAVEST LORD IS ENDED** ♪

DECISIONS

PSALM 32 v 8
The Lord says, " I will teach you the way to go; I will instruct you and advise you..."

ISAIAH Ch 6 v 8
Then I heard the Lord say, "Whom shall I send? Who will be our messenger?" "I will go. Send me!"

PROVERBS Ch 18 v 13
Listen before you answer. If you don't you are being stupid and insulting.

PSALM 73 v 24-25
You guide me with your instructions and at the end you will receive me with honour. What else have I in heaven but you? Since I have you, what else could I want on earth?

FURTHER READINGS

Proverbs Ch 16 v 1   1 Chronicles Ch 17 v 2   Proverbs Ch 6 v 20-26
Daniel Ch 10 v 12   1 Kings Ch 18 v 21

THOUGHT

Often decisions are like crossroads. If I go this way certain things could happen, if I go straight on or the other way different things will result. Sometimes there is more than one good (or bad) way and decision-making becomes even more difficult. Sometimes, decisions are made for us and not necessarily to our liking. Obedience, especially if God-given (that inner 'realisation'), is all important.

PRAYER

Allow me O God, to think through the task(s) ahead and please guide the decision which you would have me make. If it be your will, give to me a clear understanding of what you would have me do and that I then do it cheerfully as for you.

SO LET IT BE.

Inland Waterways

♪ **COME HOLY GHOST OUR SOULS INSPIRE** ♪

DIRECTIONS

ISAIAH Ch 48 v 1
. . ."I am the Lord your God, the one who wants to teach you for your own good and direct you in the way you should go . . ."

PSALM 37 v 5
Give yourself to the Lord; trust in him, and he will help you.

PSALM 25 v 4-5
Teach me your ways, O Lord; make them known unto me. Teach me to live according to your truth, for you are my God, who saves me. I always trust in you.

JAMES Ch 4 v 2-3
You strongly desire things, but you cannot get them, so you quarrel and fight. You do not have what you want because you do not ask God for it. And when you ask, you do not receive it, because your motives are bad; . . .

FURTHER READINGS

James Ch 1 v 5-6 *Proverbs Ch 3 v 5-6* *Psalm 37 v 23-24*
Psalm 16 v 7

THOUGHT

Just as a child might say "Mummy, which way is it? I am lost", so also the business executive (not so long ago a child also) might say to the board meeting - "Which way gentlemen?" - "Profit or consolidation?" - "Quality or Quantity?". Each one of us will benefit from a lifetime SIGNPOST.

PRAYER

Gracious are your ways, Heavenly Father, known so often only to yourself. Give to me please a sense of Lifetime Direction. Guide me to do only that which is good in your sight. Strengthen me in business ethics and personal relationships at all times.

SO LET IT BE.

♪ **BE THOU MY VISION O LORD** ♪
OF MY HOPE

DISCIPLINE

PSALM 119 v 75-77
I know that your judgements are righteous, Lord and that you punished me because you are faithful. Let your constant love comfort me, as you promised me, your servant. Have mercy on me and I will live because I take pleasure in your law.

PROVERBS Ch 20 v 30
Sometimes it takes a painful experience to make us change our ways.

PROVERBS Ch 3 v 11-12
When the Lord corrects you my son, pay close attention and take it as a warning. The Lord corrects those he loves, as a father corrects a son he loves.

HEBREWS Ch 12 v 5
Have you forgotten the encouraging words which God speaks to you as his sons? "My son, pay attention when the Lord corrects you, and do not be discouraged when he rebukes you . . ."

FURTHER READINGS

Proverbs Ch 13 v 24   *Proverbs Ch 3 v 12*   *Proverbs Ch 19 v 18*
Proverbs Ch 29 v 15-19

THOUGHT

Human nature often causes a positive rebellion to discipline, to be untidy not only in our actions, but also in our thinking. Very importantly the disciplined use of time fails us, we waste precious hours, we do not get down to the task at hand.

PRAYER

Lord Jesus, you know only too well the limit of lifetime available to give to us the messages of heaven, yet through discipline you achieved so much on earth in the time available to you. Give to each one of us, both in our study and in our leisure, the same sense of discipline that we may achieve great things for you.

SO LET IT BE.

Blackpool Tower & Pier

♪ **GUIDE ME O THOU GREAT JEHOVAH** ♪

DOUBT

HEBREWS Ch 1 v 6-8
But when you pray, you must believe and not doubt at all. Whoever doubts is like a wave in the sea that is driven and blown by the wind. A person . . . unable to make up his mind . . . must not think that he will receive anything from the Lord.

JOSHUA Ch 1 v 96
Don't be afraid or discouraged for I, the Lord your God, am with you wherever you go.

MARK Ch 9 v 23
Everything is possible for the person who has faith.

JOHN Ch 20 v 27
Then Jesus said to Thomas ". . . stretch out your hand and put it to my side, stop your doubting, and believe".

FURTHER READINGS

Matthew Ch 21 v 21   Hebrews Ch 13 v 8   Psalm 139 v 7-11
               Job Ch 38 v 1-3

THOUGHT

"It cannot be proven, so I don't believe it". - "Water into wine - a miracle? - I doubt it". So often we hear of something, and it is a struggle to believe the truth of it. Often too, relating to our inward faith, a little voice tells us to believe, to grasp at the unknown, yet DOUBT sets in, gets in the way, rather lets the side down, prevents us from taking that step forward.

PRAYER

Heavenly Father, are all these people right or are they wrong? Thousands have accepted you as their Lord and Master. Why Lord should that not be the same for me. Give me the ability Lord to TRUST AND OBEY, to place my trust in you, to remove any doubt and to become obedient to your call. If it is your divine will, give to me a sign of your love and care for me; yet still I will TRUST AND OBEY.

SO LET IT BE

♪ **TURN YOUR EYES UPON JESUS** ♪

ENVY

MATTHEW Ch 6 v 31-32
So do not start worrying: "Where will my food come from? or my drink? or my clothes? . . . Your Father in heaven knows that you need all these things."

GALATIANS Ch 5 v 25-26
"The Spirit has given us Life; he must also control our lives. We must not be proud or irritate one another or be jealous of one another."

EXODUS Ch 20 v 17
"Do not desire another man's house; do not desire his wife, . . . or anything that he owns."

PROVERBS Ch 24 v 1
"Don't be envious of evil people and don't try to make friends with them."

FURTHER READINGS

Hebrews Ch 13 v 5-6   Psalm 14 v 6   Proverbs Ch 14 v 30
Philippians Ch 4 v 12   James Ch 3 v 16

THOUGHT

Envy and bitterness are two destructive forces. The cash we acquire only gives to us a limited supply of all that is available, whilst so often others seem to acquire much more. No matter where we are positioned in life, to positively redirect our thinking towards those who actually have considerably less than ourselves could become the resultant cure for ENVY - a consideration by ourselves of the less fortunate, even to the extent of helping and the ensuing personal contentment that follows such action.

PRAYER

Guide me O God from the self-hurting temptation to Envy others for what they have, that I have not. You have given so much Lord, sufficient for each of us. Teach me afresh to appreciate all that I have and all that I can do for others.

SO LET IT BE

Snowdonia - N. Wales

♪ THINE BE THE GLORY ♫

FAITH

MARK Ch 9 v 23
"Yes", said Jesus, ". . . everything is possible for the person who has faith."

HEBREWS Ch 11 v 6
"No one can please God without faith, for whoever comes to God must have faith that God exists and rewards those who seek him."

ROMANS Ch 10 v 12-13
"God is the same Lord of all and richly blesses all who call to him." As the scripture says, "Everyone who calls out to the Lord for help will be saved."

JAMES Ch 2 v 24
"You see then, that it is by his actions that a person is put right with God, and not by his faith alone."

HEBREWS Ch 11 v 1-2
"To have faith is to be sure of the things we hope for, to be certain of the things we cannot see. It was by their faith that people of ancient times won God's approval."

FURTHER READINGS

Joshua Ch 1 v 7   Ephesians Ch 2 v 8-9   Isaiah Ch 7 v 9
Luke Ch 5 v 20

THOUGHT

The stock market trades under "the utmost good faith". One (money dealer) to another. They "trust" without question. The lucrative insurance contract is struck on the basis of true and faithful answers being recorded - so too our relationship with God. Faith cannot be scientifically proven, is beyond science and we should stop and consider, "Can I put my faith in mankind, or in the all-powerful Godhead?" That is the choice.

PRAYER

Faith and Trust are words you used, Heavenly Father, when teaching your disciples, our Christian forbears, how we can draw ourselves close to you. As we repent of our sins and ask your forgiveness, so also we come to you in faith on the basis of "Trust and obey, for there is no other way."

SO LET IT BE

♪ GREAT IS THY FAITHFULNESS ♫

FAMILY

PROVERBS Ch 29 v 15
"Correction and discipline are good for children. If a child has his own way, he will make his mother ashamed of him."

PROVERBS Ch 6 v 20-21
"Do what your father tells you, my son and never forget what your mother taught you. Keep their words with you always, locked in your heart."

PROVERBS Ch 20 v 7
"Children are fortunate if they have a father who is honest and does what is right."

PSALM 112 v 2
"The good man's children will be powerful in the land; his descendants will be blessed."
. . .v 4 Light shines in the darkness for good men, for those who are merciful, kind and just."

FURTHER READINGS

Joshua Ch 24 v 15   Romans Ch 12 v 10-13   Ephesians Ch 2 v 19
Psalm 68 v 5-6

THOUGHT

Family life, in the main, brings great joy and happiness: The birth of a child, the marriage of a young couple, success at work or University, the joy of meeting up after a prolonged separation. The special occasion dinner table laden with extra foods. Even the fulfilment of a lifetime's work and commencing retirement. Events that we share yet we can so often take for granted.

PRAYER

Thank you Lord for our families and our friends. Give each one of us the strength to do that which is right, so as never to upset the other members in any disappointing way. Protect O Lord, those with almost no family, or whose families are torn apart through unnecessary hurt. Help us into the family church of God.

SO LET IT BE.

Marshwood Parish Church - Dorset

♪ **WHO IS ON THE LORD'S SIDE** ♫

FEAR

PSALM 23 v 4
"Even if I go through the deepest darkness, I will not be afraid Lord, for you are with me, your shepherd's rod and staff protect me."

MARK Ch 4 v 41
But they were terribly afraid and said to one another, "Who is this man? Even the wind and the waves obey him."

PSALM 27 v 1
"The Lord is my light and my salvation; I will fear no one. The Lord protects me from all danger; I will never be afraid ......I will still trust God."

PROVERBS Ch 9 v 12
"You are the one who will profit if you have wisdom, and if you reject it, you are the one who will suffer."

HEBREWS Ch 13 v 5-6
For God has said, "I will never leave you; I will never abandon you" Let us be bold, then, and say, "The Lord is my helper."

FURTHER READINGS

John Ch 4 v 18   Romans Ch 8 v 15   Isaiah Ch 41 v 10
1 John Ch 4 v 18

THOUGHT

Daniel must have been almost consumed with fear, sitting in the den of lions, yet he had faith in his God. Fear can sometimes overrule our clear thinking, yet God knows in every detail the fear which overtakes us for whatever reason. He too can guide us into a fearless time again, but ONLY if we call upon him.

PRAYER

Lord God I can feel you reaching out to me at this worrying time and the knowledge is of deep comfort. Quieten my fear Lord, dispel my worry, and give to me a fresh assurance for the future.

SO LET IT BE.

♪ **YESTERDAY, TODAY, FOREVER** ♫

FORGIVENESS

COLOSSIANS Ch 3 v 13
Be tolerant with one another and forgive one another whenever any of you has a complaint against someone else. You must forgive one another just as God has forgiven you.

2 CORINTHIANS Ch 5 v 19
God was making all mankind his friends through Christ. God did not keep an account of their sins, and he has given us the message which tells how he makes them his friends.

EPHESIANS Ch 4 v 31-32
Get rid of bitterness. No more shouting and insults, no more hateful feelings of any sort. Instead be kind and tender-hearted to one another, and forgive one another, as God has forgiven you through Christ.

FURTHER READINGS

Matthew Ch 18 v 21-22   Acts Ch 13 v 38-39   John Ch 8 v 31-32
1 John Ch 1 v 19

THOUGHT

When Christ's hands were nailed to the cross, absolute forgiveness became available to all who truly repented of their sins. However, individually each one of us has to ask.

PRAYER

You taught us yourself Lord, to pray for our own forgiveness, just as we do forgive the sins of others. Grant that these words be true, deep from my heart Lord, and not just meaningless poetry.

SO LET IT BE.

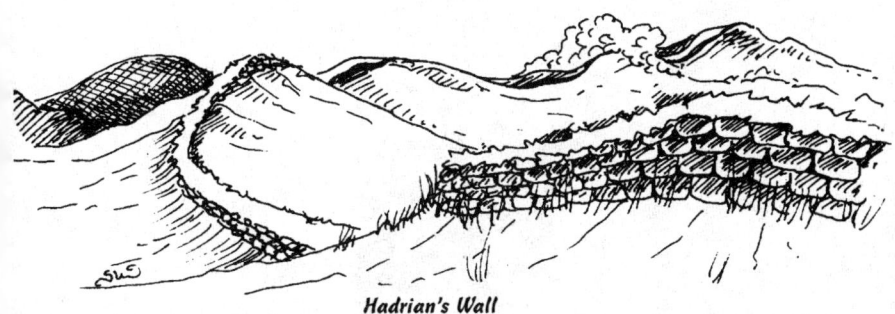

Hadrian's Wall

♪ THERE'S A WAY BACK TO GOD ♫

FRIENDSHIP

JOHN Ch 15 v 12-14
My commandment is this; Love one another, just as I love you. The greatest love a person can have for his friends, is to give his life for them, and you are my friends if you do what I command you.

PROVERBS Ch 17 v 17
Friends always show their love. What are friends for if not to share trouble?

PROVERBS Ch 18 v 24
Some friendships do not last, but some friends are more loyal than brothers.

PROVERBS Ch 27 v 10
Do not forget your friends, or your father's friends. If you are in trouble, don't ask your brothers for help; a neighbour nearby can help you more than a brother who is far away.

FURTHER READINGS

Proverbs Ch 18 v 19   1 John Ch 4 v 19-21   Matthew Ch 5 v 23-24
James Ch 4 v 4   Romans Ch 5 v 10-11

THOUGHT

Enemies of God we could have been! But through Jesus the chance of eternal friendship - just through the sincerity of asking.

PRAYER

For the friendships I have, I thank you Lord God. Allow me the strength of character to feel this way for everyone I meet, regardless of circumstances, because sometimes Lord, you know the difficulty this causes me.

SO LET IT BE

♪ **WHAT A FRIEND WE HAVE IN JESUS** ♫

FRUSTRATION

GALATIANS Ch 6 v 9
So let us not become tired of doing good; for if we do not give up, the time will come when we will reap the harvest.

PROVERBS Ch 27 v 3
The weight of stone and sand is nothing compared to the trouble that stupidity can cause.

PSALM 37 v 4-5
Seek your happiness in the Lord, and he will give you your heart's desire. Give yourself to the Lord; trust in him, and he will help you.

JOB Ch 3 v 23
God keeps their future hidden and hems them in on every side.

PHILIPPIANS Ch 3 v 12
I do not claim that I have already succeeded or have already become perfect . . . Keep striving to win the prize for which Christ Jesus has already won us to himself.

FURTHER READINGS

Psalm 32 v 3-5   Psalm 31 v 7   1 Timothy Ch 1 v 30-4
                    Hebrews Ch 12 v 1b

THOUGHT

Thomas Carlyle once said, "Our grand business is not to see what lies dimly at a distance, but to do what lies clearly at hand". Frustration sometimes causes much hurt, but it is worth remembering that "evil triumphs when good men do nothing" and doing something often eases the current difficulty.

PRAYER

Lord God at times frustration wells up within us, causing inability to do as we should, and sometimes others have not done as they should have done. Give me grace that patience can overide this frustration, and that good become the final outcome.

SO LET IT BE

The New Forest - Hampshire

♪ **BE STILL AND KNOW THAT I AM GOD** ♫

GOD'S DAY

GENESIS Ch 1 v 31; Ch 2 v 1-3a
God looked at everything he had made, and was very pleased . . . and so the whole universe was completed. By the seventh day God finished what he had been doing and stopped working. He blessed the seventh day and set it apart as a special day.

MARK Ch 2 v 27
And Jesus concluded, "The Sabbath was made for the good of man; man was not made for the Sabbath."

ROMANS Ch 14 v 5
(Whilst) one person thinks that a certain day is more important than other days, someone else thinks that all days are the same . . . whoever thinks highly of a certain day does so in honour of the Lord.

EXODUS Ch 20 v 8-10
Observe the Sabbath and keep it holy. You have six days in which to do your work, but the seventh day is a day of rest dedicated to me.

FURTHER READINGS

Revelation Ch 1 v 10   Matthew Ch 12 v 8-13   Isaiah Ch 58 v 13-14
Colossians Ch 2 v 16-17

THOUGHT
Sunday sport, Sunday Supermarkets etc., etc. Where does all this stand in the plan of God Almighty? In this hectic world do we slow down regularly and take stock of the what, why, when and how and of our individual timing in this plan? If we are going to love God, we must give him a little time each day, and also on the planned day of rest.

PRAYER
Guard us Heavenly Father, lest we be in pursuit of wealth alone. Remind us constantly that our time span on earth is short. Help us O God to regularly take time out to consider your ways, to give thanks to you, to make our repentance and to be seeking to do that which you want or would have us do at all times.

SO LET IT BE.

♪ **ALLELUIA - GIVE THANKS TO** ♫
THE RISEN LORD

GOD'S PURPOSE

ROMANS Ch 8 v 28
We know that in all things God works for good with those who love him, those whom he has called according to his purpose.

EPHESIANS Ch 1 v 5
Because of his love God had already decided that through Jesus Christ he would make us his sons - This was his pleasure and purpose.
Ch 1 v 7
For by the death of Christ we are set free, that is, our sins are forgiven. How great is the grace of God, which he gave to us in such large measure.
Ch 1 v 10
This plan which God will complete when the time is right, is to bring all creation together, everything in heaven and on earth, with Christ as head.

FURTHER READINGS

Psalm 18 v 30 *Galatians Ch 1 v 4* *Psalm 19 v 7*
Romans Ch 5 v 6 *Ephesians Ch 1 v 11*

THOUGHT
Many believe that God has two dwellings, one in heaven, and the other in every meek and thankful heart. There is a famous picture of Christ knocking on the outside of the door - the door of your heart. The joy upon opening this door can be yours if only you will allow it to happen.

PRAYER
God you have given us Life and you have shown us purpose through scripture and through Jesus Christ. Give to us a meek and thankful heart, that we can fulfil our portion of the wondrous task set before us. Make us strong in life, and strong also in fulfilling your wonderful purpose.

SO LET IT BE.

Norfolk Broads

♪ **STAND UP, STAND UP FOR JESUS** ♫

GUILT

ROMANS Ch 3 v 23-24
Everyone has sinned and is far away from God's saving presence. But by the free gift of God's grace all are put right with him through Jesus Christ, who sets them free.

1 JOHN Ch 3 v 20
If our conscience condemns us, we know that God is greater than our conscience and that he knows everything.
Ch 3 v 23
What God commands is that we believe in his Son Jesus Christ and love one another, just as Jesus Christ commanded us.

ROMANS Ch 8 v 1
There is no condemnation now for those who live in union with Jesus Christ.

FURTHER READINGS

1 John Ch 1 v 8-9   James Ch 2 v 10   Psalm 51 v 3
Lamentations Ch 2 v 20a

THOUGHT

"The vilest offender who truly believes, (repents), that moment from Jesus, a pardon receives."
AN ABSOLUTE PROMISE, NO MATTER WHO, WHEN, WHAT OR WHY.
Punishment on earth may still be needed, but a pardon from God is absolute if truly repentant.

PRAYER

O God in heaven, you gave your son Jesus to die upon the Cross, that everyone's sins, but especially my sins O God might be forgiven and forgotten for ever. I ask not only forgiveness of what I have done wrong, but the strength and determination never to do likewise again.

SO LET IT BE

♪ **SING A NEW SONG TO THE LORD** ♫

HEAVEN

JOHN Ch 10 v 27-28
Jesus said, . . . "My sheep (people) listen to my voice; I know them, and they follow me. I give them eternal life, and they shall never die . . . "

MATTHEW Ch 7 v 13-14
. . . "The gate to hell is wide, and the road to it is easy, and there are many who travel it. But the gate to life (eternal) is narrow and the way that leads to it is hard . . ."

2 CORINTHIANS Ch 5 v 1
For we know that when this tent we live in - our body here on earth - is torn down, God will have a house in heaven for us to live in, a home he himself has made and which will last forever . . .(5b) and he gave us his Spirit as the guarantee of all that he has in store for us.

FURTHER READINGS

Colossians Ch 3 v 1-4   1 Corinthians Ch 15 v 51-54   Luke Ch 20 v 34-36
Deuteronomy Ch 26 v 15   Nehemiah Ch 9 v 6

THOUGHT
No eye has seen, no ear has heard, no mind has conceived that which God has prepared for those who love him. A place, in other words, beyond our wildest imagination. Yes - a place beyond the very best we have ever heard of.

PRAYER
Open our hearts Heavenly Father to an unfailing belief in the promises made to all mankind. If we trust and obey, you'll show us no other way than the pathway to eternal life to be by your side. Heavenly Father walk closely beside me along life's precarious path that I may never falter on the journey.

SO LET IT BE.

Isle of Wight

♪ HOLY HOLY HOLY LORD GOD ALMIGHTY ♫

HELL

LUKE Ch 16 v 22-24
The poor man died, and was carried by the angels to sit beside Abraham at the feast in heaven. The rich man died and was buried, and in Hades (Hell), where he was in great pain, he looked up and saw Abraham far away, with Lazarus the poor man at his side. He called out - "Take pity on me, send Lazarus to dip his finger in some water and cool my tongue, because I am in great pain in this fire (of Hell)."

THESSALONIANS Ch 1 v 8a
. . . Those who reject God and who do not obey the Good News about our Lord Jesus, will suffer the punishment of eternal destruction separated from the presence of the Lord and from his glorious might.

MATTHEW Ch 25 v 41
"Away from me, you that are under God's curse! Away to the eternal fire which has been prepared for the Devil and all his angels!"

FURTHER READINGS
2 Thessalonians Ch 1 v 8-9   Matthew Ch 25 v 45   Revelation Ch 20 v 14-15
Matthew Ch 13 v 41-42

THOUGHT
Disbelieve hell and you unscrew, unsettle and unpin everything in scripture. If heaven is a place too wonderful to imagine, then hell - the direct opposite, must be appalling, terrible. - More than just a thought!

PRAYER
Heavenly Father, it is so easy to neglect serious concern for our own long-term well-being, to disregard the immense suffering, that eternal destruction will give to those who care not. Help me urgently Lord God, to seek your ways and a full repentance of my sins and mistakes. From now on hold me closely day by day.

SO LET IT BE

♪ REVIVE THY WORK, O LORD ♫

HONESTY

2 TIMOTHY Ch 2 v 19
But the solid foundation which God has laid cannot be shaken; and on it are written these words, "The Lord knows who are his." and "Whoever says that he belongs to the Lord must turn away from wrongdoing."

DEUTERONOMY Ch 25 v 13-14
"Do not cheat when you use weights and measures" . . . (16) The Lord hates people who cheat.

PROVERBS Ch 16 v 8
It is better to have a little honestly earned, than to have a large income gained dishonestly.

PROVERBS Ch 10 v 29
The Lord protects honest people, but destroys those who do wrong.

FURTHER READINGS

Luke Ch 16 v 10 Romans Ch 12 v 17 Psalm 5 v 6
Proverbs Ch 28 v 18

THOUGHT
Honesty is the first chapter in the book of wisdom. The true test is when we do not do dishonestly that which we knew we would never be caught doing - an in-built TRIUMPH!

PRAYER
God, you who have provided us with temptation that we might be tested in your sight, give us at all times the honesty you require, that we may be found acceptable at the time we come face to face before you. Please give to us no more temptation than that which we can bravely overcome.

SO LET IT BE.

The Lake District

♪ HOW SWEET THE NAME OF JESUS ♪ SOUNDS

JOY

ROMANS Ch 4 v 7-8
"Happy are those whose wrongs are forgiven, whose sins are pardoned! Happy is the person whose sins the Lord will not keep account of."

1 THESSALONIANS Ch 5 v 16-18
Be joyful always, pray at all times, be thankful in all circumstances. This is what God wants from you in your life in union with Jesus Christ.

PSALM 1 v 2
. . . they find joy in obeying the law of the Lord.

PSALM 30 v 5
Tears may flow in the night, but joy comes in the morning.

JOHN Ch 15 v 9
I love you just as my Father (God) loves me, . . . (v11) "I have told you this so that my joy may be in you and that your joy may be complete."

FURTHER READINGS

Luke Ch 2 v 10   2 Corinthians Ch 4 v 18   Romans Ch 14 v 17
Nehemiah Ch 8 v 10b

THOUGHT

There is no duty we so much like to undertake as the duty of being happy and by being happy we sow anonymous benefits upon the world. Give to at least one person today one of your precious smiles. This kindness will cost you nothing, yet it will bring joy to your heart, as well as theirs.

PRAYER

Your angels proclaimed "GREAT JOY to all the people". Lord, grant that we may ever walk closer in your presence, and contain that absolute joy in our hearts until you call us into your own. Help me to smile more often Lord, to think positive thoughts, and to express great joy whenever possible.

SO LET IT BE.

♪ **JESUS! THE NAME HIGH OVER ALL** ♫

LAW

JAMES Ch 1 v 25
. . . Whoever looks closely into the perfect law that sets people free, who keeps on paying attention to it and does not simply listen and then forget it, but puts it into practice - that person will be blessed by God in what he does.

ROMANS Ch 13 v 1b
Everyone must obey the state authorities, because no authority exists without God's permission, and the existing authorities have been put there by God.

GALATIANS Ch 3 v 19a
What, then, was the purpose of the Law? It was added in order to show what wrong doing is, and it was meant to last until the coming of Abrahams descendant, to whom the promise was made.
v 21b
For if mankind had received a law that could bring life, then everyone could be put right with God by obeying it.

MATTHEW Ch 22 v 21
So Jesus said to them, . . . "Pay the Emperor what belongs to the Emperor, and pay God what belongs to God."

FURTHER READINGS

Psalm 119 v 36   *Matthew Ch 5 v 19b*   *Psalm 19 v 7*
Psalm 1 v1-6

THOUGHT
What is hateful to you, do not do to another. That is the whole law and all else is explanation.

PRAYER
We pray for obedience Lord to those ten precious laws you have made known to us, your commandments, that we may seek eternal salvation through lawful citizenship with you.

SO LET IT BE.

Giant's Causeway - Co. Antrim

♪ **ASCRIBE GREATNESS TO OUR GOD THE ROCK** ♫

LONELINESS

PSALM 25 v 16
Turn to me Lord, and be merciful to me, because I am lonely and weak.

MATTHEW Ch 28 v 20 b
Jesus drew near and said, . . . "I will be with you always, to the end of the age."

JOB Ch 11 v 9
God's greatness is broader than the earth, wider than the sea . . .
v 15
Face the world again, firm and courageous. Then all your troubles will fade from your memory.
v 18
. . . God said "It is not good for the man to live alone, I will make a suitable companion to help him."

FURTHER READINGS

Revelation Ch 3 v 20   *John Ch 16 v 31-33*   *Psalm 40 v 1*
Psalm 32 v 8   *Ecclesiastes Ch 4 v 9-10*

THOUGHT

Physically, we may be alone, yet within each one of us is the opportunity to talk with God. Start with a little chat, tell him what your concerns are and perhaps you will find these chats leading into prayer. Loneliness will dissipate. Maybe followed through with an action, getting involved locally, talking to a neighbour - asking them what their concerns are and even using the phone numbers within this book (Page 62).

PRAYER

Loneliness is something, Lord Jesus, which you must have known in your time on earth. Help me with your precious understanding, that I may feel your love and your closeness and be drawn away from my present feeling of isolation.

SO LET IT BE.

♪ **I AM TRUSTING THEE LORD JESUS** ♪

LOVE

1 CORINTHIANS Ch 12 v 4-8a
Love is patient and kind; it is not jealous or conceited or proud; Love is not ill-mannered or selfish or irritable; Love does not keep a record of wrongs; Love is not happy with evil, but is happy with the truth. Love never gives up, and its faith, hope and patience never fail. Love is eternal.

LUKE Ch 14 v 26
(Jesus said . . .) "Whoever comes to me cannot be my disciple unless he loves me more than he loves his father and mother, his wife, his children, his brothers and sisters, and himself as well".

EXODUS Ch 20 v 6
But I (God) show my love to thousands of generations of those who love me and obey my laws.

JOHN Ch 13 v 34
". . . Now I (Jesus) give you a new commandment: Love one another. As I have loved you, so you must love one another."

FURTHER READINGS

1 John Ch 4 v 7; Ch 5 v 3	Isaiah Ch 44 v 2	Leviticus Ch 19 v 18
1 Corinthians Ch 13 v 1-13	Galatians Ch 5 v 22-23	Matthew Ch 5 v 43-46

THOUGHT
A simple analysis 1) Love towards the risen Lord; 2) Love of a parent/child; 3) Romantic love of a partner; and 4) Love of a commodity or a job. Each especially heartfelt, yet controlled and dealt with in different ways.

PRAYER
Dear God in heaven, who has given us the ability to love and be loved; may we not only enjoy and understand this precious gift of love from others to ourselves, but be even more generous in our giving of love to others, especially where we might not normally be so.

Epping Forest

♩ O LOVE THAT WILL NOT LET ME GO ♫

NEEDS

MATTHEW Ch 6 v 31
Jesus was teaching . . . "So do not start worrying; 'where will my food come from? or my drink? or my clothes?' . . . Your Father in heaven knows that you need all these things."

PSALM 31 v 19
How wonderful are the good things you keep for those who honour you! How securely you protect those who trust you.

PSALM 104 v 24
Lord, you have made so many things, how wisely you have made them all.
v 27-28
All of them depend on you to give them food when they need it. You give it to them . . . and they are satisfied.

MATTHEW Ch 7 v 11b
How much more then, will your Father in heaven give good things to those who ask him.

FURTHER READINGS

Luke Ch 11 v 2-3   Philippians Ch 4 v 11-13   Job Ch 1 v 21
2 Corinthians Ch 9 v 8

THOUGHT

Confusing it so often is, that what we think we need, you well know we need not. Whilst we need a water tank in the loft, the real need for thousands of families in other countries is simply for water to come out of the ground.

PRAYER

Help us Lord God, to more accurately distinguish our needs from our wants. Continue in your loving provision to supply our needs and provide others with their needs before attending to our wants. This we pray in your name.

SO LET IT BE.

♪ **IMMORTAL, INVISIBLE, GOD ONLY WISE** ♫

PATIENCE

JAMES Ch 5 v 7
Be patient then my brothers, until the Lord comes. See how patient a farmer is as he waits for his land to produce precious corn.

ROMANS Ch 15 v 5
May God, the source of patience and encouragement, enable you to have the same ... among yourselves by following the example of Christ Jesus.

EPHESIANS Ch 4 v 2
Be always humble, gentle and patient. Show your love by being tolerant with one another.

JAMES Ch 1 v 4
Make sure that your endurance (and patience) carries you all the way without failing, so that you may be perfect and complete, lacking nothing.

FURTHER READINGS

Psalm 40 v 1   *Psalm 37 v 7a*   *Hebrews Ch 10 v 36*
Romans Ch 5 v 3-5

THOUGHT
A little reminder that when temptation allows us to lose our temper, it is then that we start letting other people down. Often patience alone will begin to put things right.

PRAYER
O God, grant me the courage to change what I can change, the patience to endure what I cannot change, and the wisdom to know and understand the difference.

SO LET IT BE.

The Yorkshire Dales

♪ THE KING OF LOVE MY SHEPHERD IS ♪

PEACE

JOHN Ch 16 v 33b
...You will have peace by being united with me. The world will make you suffer, but be brave! I have defeated the world!

JOHN Ch 14 v 27
"Peace is what I leave with you, it is my peace that I give you. I do not give it as the world does. Do not be worried or upset; do not be afraid."

PSALM 23 v 4
Even if I go through the deepest darkness, I will not be afraid, O Lord, for you are with me.

ROMANS Ch 5 v 1b-2
...We have peace with God through our Lord Jesus Christ. He has brought us by faith into this experience of God's grace.

FURTHER READINGS

Psalm 34 v 14   Psalm 85 v 10   Philippians Ch 4 v 6-7
Numbers Ch 6 v 24-26

THOUGHT
The shortest route to world peace is through world cooperation. The shortest route to domestic and marital peace is through communication. "It's good to talk", nation to nation, company to company, and individual to individual.

PRAYER
Give to mankind Lord God, the wisdom and ability to talk, not to argue, that peaceful solutions be found no matter how grand or how trivial the situation may be. Save us from the disharmony we so easily provoke against ourselves.

SO LET IT BE

♫ I'VE GOT PEACE LIKE A RIVER ♫

PRAISE

PSALM 9 v 1-2
I will praise you, Lord, with all my heart; I will tell of the wonderful things you have done. I will sing with joy because of you. I will sing praise to you Almighty God.

EPHESIANS Ch 5 v 19
Speak to one another with words of psalms, hymns and sacred songs; sing hymns and psalms to the Lord with praise in your hearts.

PSALM 106 v 1-2
Give thanks to the Lord, because he is good; his love is eternal. Who can tell all the great things he has done? Who can praise him enough?

PSALM 47 v1
Clap your hands with joy, all peoples! Praise God with long songs.

FURTHER READINGS

Psalm 37 v 10a   Psalm 16 v 7-8   1 Thessalonians Ch 5 v 16-17
2 Corinthians Ch 2 v 14a

THOUGHT

It has been said that, "Man should utter a hundred daily praises to God", and that man's chief work is ... "The praise of God." A little praise often turns losers into winners. It costs absolutely nothing to give a little genuine, well-earned praise - try it!

PRAYER

Praise my soul the King of Heaven; To his feet thy tribute bring;
Ransomed, healed, restored, forgiven, Who like thee his praise should sing.
Praise him, praise him, Praise him, praise him,
Praise the everlasting King.   Henry Lyte.

SO LET IT BE.

Tower Bridge - London

♪ PRAISE TO THE HOLIEST ♫

PRAYER

HEBREWS Ch 13 v 21
May the God of Peace provide you with every good thing you need in order to do his will, and may he, through Jesus Christ, do in us what pleases him.

MATTHEW Ch 18 v 19
Jesus told his disciples ... "Whenever two of you on earth agree about anything you pray for, it will be done for you by my Father in heaven."

JAMES Ch 5 v 16
Confess your sins to one another and pray for one another, so that you will be healed. The prayer of a good person has a powerful effect.

ROMANS Ch 8 v 16-28
The Spirit also comes to help us, weak as we are. For we do not know how we ought to pray; the Spirit himself pleads with God for us ... and God sees into our hearts, knows what the thought of the Spirit is ... and we know that in all things God works for good with those who love him.

FURTHER READINGS

John Ch 15 v 7   Matthew Ch 6 v 7-15   Psalm 102 v 1-2

THOUGHT

Prayer is never the word spoken or read from text, unless it always represents an outpouring from the heart. We cannot, nor should we ever try, to cheat God.

PRAYER

Lord God, you have taught us in person and on earth, how to pray, and simply too. Give to our hearts a deep sincerity of the words we choose in prayer and conversation with you, that you may hear us and bless us on our way for you.

SO LET IT BE.

♪ **PRAYER IS THE SOULS SINCERE DESIRE** ♪

PROBLEMS

JAMES Ch 1 v 2-3
... Consider yourselves fortunate when all kinds of troubles come your way, for you know that when your faith succeeds in facing such trials, the result is the ability to endure.

PSALM 77 v 1-2
I cry aloud to God; I cry aloud and he hears me. In times of trouble I pray to the Lord.

PSALM 71 v 20-21
You have sent troubles and suffering upon me, but you will restore my strength ... You will make me greater than ever, you will comfort me again.

2 CORINTHIANS Ch 4 v 8-9
... often troubled, but not crushed; sometimes in doubt, but never in despair; there are many enemies, but we are never without a friend, and though badly hurt at times, we are not destroyed.

v 18
For we fix our attention, not on things that are seen, but on things unseen. What can be seen lasts only for a time, but what cannot be seen lasts for ever.

FURTHER READINGS

1 Peter Ch 4 v 12-13   *Romans Ch 5 v 3-5*   *Nahum Ch 1 v 7*
Psalm 34 v 8

THOUGHT
One of the Devil's favourite tricks is in setting problems against us, which we think are just too great. Don't fall for it; think and pray. Then think and pray again. With sincerity you will win, not the Devil.

PRAYER
Problems are not new to you God. Help us to accept that the problems given in each instance are a part of your purpose and guide us accordingly to the right conclusion.

SO LET IT BE.

Welsh Valleys

♫ REACH OUT AND TOUCH THE LORD ♫

RICHES

PROVERBS Ch 16 v 8
It is better to have a little, honestly earned, than to have a large income gained dishonestly.

MATTHEW Ch 6 v 19-20
"Do not store up riches for yourself here on earth, where moths and dust destroy, and robbers break in and steal. Instead store up riches for yourself in heaven ... for your heart will always be where your riches are."

MARK Ch 10 v 21
Jesus looked straight at him with love and said, "You need only one thing. Go and sell all you have and give the money to the poor, and you will have riches in heaven; then come and follow me."

1 TIMOTHY Ch 6 v 7-9
What did we bring into the world? Nothing! So then if we have food and clothes, that should be enough for us. But those who want to get rich fall into temptation and are caught in the trap of many foolish and harmful desires...

FURTHER READINGS

2 Corinthians Ch 12 v 15   Philippians Ch 4 v 12-13   Psalm 62 v10
Proverbs Ch 11 v 4

THOUGHT

It was once said, "Money will buy a pretty good dog but it won't buy the wag of his tail," and "... how much harder" Jesus himself told us ... "For a rich man to enter the Kingdom of God."

PRAYER

Lord God, help me never to be a slave of money, guide me to give in such a way as makes you smile. Teach me to be a good steward of what you have made available to me.

SO LET IT BE.

♫ **WE REALLY WANT TO THANK YOU LORD** ♫

SEX

1 CORINTHIANS Ch 6 v 13b
... The body is not to be used for immorality, but to serve the Lord; and the Lord provides for the body.
v 18
... Avoid immorality, any other sin a man commits does not affect his body; but the man who is guilty of sexual immorality sins against his own body.

PROVERBS Ch 5 v 18-19
Be happy with your wife and find joy with this girl whom you married - pretty and graceful ... let her charms keep you happy; let her surround you with her love.

COLOSSIANS Ch 3 v 18-19
Wives, submit to your husbands for that is what you should do as Christians. Husbands love your wives and do not be harsh with them.

FURTHER READINGS

Proverbs Ch 7 v 6-7   *Proverbs Ch 31 v 10*   *Matthew Ch 19 v 4-6*
Corinthians Ch 7 v 32-34   *Job Ch 31 v1*

THOUGHT

There is without doubt a great attraction between male and female human beings; just part of an amazing God-given creation. The drawing together of two people for lifetime companionship should never be taken lightly. Sexuality differs greatly person to person, and far better that you fully understand yourself in life first, long before a commitment to another.

PRAYER

Lord God, give me your guidance that I might be able to choose the right friends and relationships, that I will always be as concerned and truthful towards others as I would wish of them towards me. Strengthen the control of myself over my feelings. Lord God, keep my actions correct at all times.

SO LET IT BE.

Stonehenge

♪ IN MY LIFE LORD BE GLORIFIED ♫

SHARING

MATTHEW Ch 6 v 42
When someone asks you for something, give it to him; When someone wants to borrow something, lend it to him (or her).

MATTHEW Ch 7 v 3
When you help a needy person, do it in such a way that even your closest friends will not know about it ... it will be a private matter, and your father, who sees what you do in private, will reward you.

LUKE Ch 6 v 30
Give to everyone who asks you for something, and when someone takes what is yours, do not ask for it back. Do for others just what you want them to do for you.

PROVERBS Ch 11 v 25
Be generous, and you will be prosperous. Help others, and you will be helped.

FURTHER READINGS

2 Corinthians Ch 9 v 7-9   *Proverbs Ch 22 v 9*   *Proverbs Ch 19 v 17*
Acts Ch 20 v 35   *Romans Ch 12 v 13*

THOUGHT

An unknown writer once said, "Give according to your income lest God make your income according to your giving."
A joke untold remains lonely until it is shared with another; so too is the human being.

PRAYER

Lord God, so often we haven't enough, we want more, until for a moment or two we think of those in very poor countries, whose real need is their next meal and next drink of water. Teach us the difference between want and actual need, and make us constantly aware of the need to share that which you have already provided us with in the first place.

SO LET IT BE.

♪ **BIND US TOGETHER LORD** ♫

SIN

PSALM 103 v 12
As far as the east is from the west, so far does God remove our sins from us.

1 JOHN Ch 1 v 8-9
If we say we have no sin, we deceive ourselves, and there is no truth in us. But if we confess our sins to God, he will keep his promise and do what is right: he will forgive us our sins and purify us from all our wrongdoing.

PSALM 34 v 12-14
Would you like to enjoy life? ... then hold back from speaking evil and from telling lies ... turn away from evil and do good; strive for peace with all your heart.

ROMANS Ch 6 v 12
Sin must no longer rule in your mortal bodies, so that you obey the desires of your natural self. Nor must you surrender any parts of yourselves to sin to be used for wicked purposes. Instead, give yourselves to God, as those who have been brought from death to life, and surrender your whole being to him to be used for righteous purposes.

FURTHER READINGS

James Ch 4 v 7-10   *2 Peter Ch 2 v 20-21*   *James Ch 4 v 17*
Romans Ch 5 v 12

THOUGHT
Sin became part of man since the earliest of times. Sin and the temptation to sin escapes no one. The Devil takes great delight each time we falter. Our every act of sin is his success. We need a constant twenty-four hour security guard at all times.

PRAYER
Father God, you chose to make sin a part of your creation. You also make it possible for each and every one of us to overcome the temptation of doing wrong. Give us the continuing strength to not falter, lest we fall into the ploy of the Devil. This prayer we ask in your holy name.

SO LET IT BE.

The North Cornish Coast

♪ **DEAR LORD AND FATHER OF MANKIND** ♫

SORROW

2 CORINTHIANS Ch 7 v 10
For the sadness that is used by God, brings a change of heart that leads to salvation - and there is no regret in that! But sadness that is merely human causes death.

ROMANS Ch 12 v 12
Let your hope keep you joyful, be patient in your troubles, and pray at all times ...
v 15-16
Weep with those who weep. Have the same concern for everyone.

PSALM 5 v 1
Listen to my words, O Lord, and hear my sighs. Listen to my cry for help, my God and King.

ISAIAH Ch 51 v 11
Those whom you (God) have rescued will reach Jerusalem with gladness, singing and shouting for joy. They will be happy forever, for ever free from sorrow and grief.

FURTHER READINGS

Job Ch 14 v 1　　*John Ch 14 v 1-4*　　*Psalm 33 v 18-19*
2 Corinthians Ch 4 v 16-18

THOUGHT
Whilst the passing of time itself becomes a healing for sadness, nevertheless in times of grief a soothing remedy is the closeness of a kind and honest friend. Each of us will be called upon from time to time to give of ourselves to others in distress.

PRAYER
Father God in heaven, you have planned your world with so much joy, but necessarily a little sorrow too. Succour and help those in their sadness, may they become closely aware of your love and support as the damage heals. We make this prayer to you Lord.

SO LET IT BE.

♪ JESUS SHALL REIGN ♫
WHERE'ERE THE SUN

SUFFERING

ROMANS CH 8 v 17
Since we are his children, we will possess the blessings he keeps for his people, and will also possess with Christ what God has kept for him: for if we share in Christ's suffering, we will also share his glory.

HEBREWS Ch 5 v 8
But even though Jesus was God's son, he learnt through suffering to be obedient.

2 CORINTHIANS Ch 12 v 17
... I prayed to the Lord ... but his answer was, "My grace is all you need, for my power is strongest when you are weak."

JOB Ch 36 v 8-11
But if people are bound in chains, suffering for what they have done, God shows them their sins and their pride. He makes them listen to his warning to turn away from evil. If they obey God and serve him, they (will then) live out their lives in peace and prosperity.

FURTHER READINGS

Psalm 121 v 1-2   James Ch 1 v 27   Job Ch 15 v 11
                       Job Ch 30 v 16

THOUGHT

"Under sufferance" when someone else wants it done their way, or in a different way to our own thinking, is the frequent cry of young people. Sometimes also we put up with a situation not of our choosing because it will be pleasing to someone else. Patient sufferance is a virtue of maturity.

PRAYER

Lord God, we know we cannot always have our own way, especially when trying to please and help others. Give to us the strength of character to do as you would have us do and to put up with every kind of suffering as though we were acting for you.

SO LET IT BE.

The 'Backs' - Cambridge

♪ MY SOUL DOTH MAGNIFY THE LORD ♫

TALENTS

ROMANS Ch 12 v 6
We are to use our different gifts in accordance with the grace God has given us (v 8) ... Whoever shares with others should do it generously ...

COLOSSIANS Ch 3 v 23
Whatever you do, work at it with all your heart, as though you were working for the Lord and not for men.

1 PETER Ch 4 v 10
Each one (of us), also a manager of God's different gifts, must use for the good of others the special gift he (she) has received from God.

COLOSSIANS Ch 3 v 16
Christ's message in all its richness must live in your hearts. Teach and instruct each other in wisdom. Sing psalms, hymns and sacred songs; sing to God with thanksgiving in your hearts.

FURTHER READINGS

Romans Ch 2 v 6-11   *Galatians Ch 6 v 3-5*   *Ephesians Ch 5 v 16-17*
1 Corinthians Ch 6 v 19

THOUGHT

Just as with an athlete in training, the more we practice the specific skills given to us, the better we become at perfecting the task. We need to do what we can, with what we have, and where we are - a creative development of talent.

PRAYER

Help me to use my body and my brain, Lord, to the very best of my ability. Give me an understanding that no matter how good and honest a job it may be, it not only supplies my needs but it also serves a purpose for mankind. If, Lord God, you need me to change, please give to me a sign and show me the way.

SO LET IT BE.

♪ NOW THANK WE ALL OUR GOD ♪

TEMPTATION

1 CORINTHIANS Ch 10 v 12-13
Whoever thinks he is standing firm had better be careful that he does not fall. Every test that you have experienced is the kind that normally comes to people. But God keeps his promise, and he will not allow you to be tested beyond your power to remain firm; at the time you are put to the test, he will give you the strength to endure it, and so provide you with a way out.

JAMES Ch 1 v 12
Happy is the person who remains faithful under trials, because when he succeeds in passing such a test, he will receive as his reward the life which God has promised to those who love him.

1 JOHN Ch 2 v 16-17
Everything that belongs to the world - what the sinful self desires, what people see and want and everything in this world that people are so proud of - none of this comes from the Father; it all comes from the world. The world and everything in it that people desire is passing away; but he who does the will of God lives for ever.

FURTHER READINGS

Romans Ch 3 v 22-23 *Titus Ch 1 v 15* *Hebrews Ch 10 v 26*
1 Thessalonians Ch 5 v 21

THOUGHT
Regardless of whether rich and famous, or hungry and poor, we all equally suffer the temptation to go astray. Yes, the devil attacks each and every one of us delighting at any slip we make. Shall we help the Devil? or shall we serve God?

PRAYER
Heavenly Father we read in scripture of how you knew well the crafty ways of the Devil and how he tempted you with great offers of help and alleviance of suffering. Give to each of us the ability to triumph over sin and to defend ourselves against the constant temptations the devil presents to us all.

SO LET IT BE

The twisted Tower - Chesterfield

♪ **OPEN OUR EYES LORD, WE WANT TO SEE JESUS**

TIME

PSALM 90 v 12
Teach us how short our life is, so that we may become wise.

LUKE Ch 12 v 40
. . . You too must be ready, because the Son of Man will come at an hour when you are not expecting him.

MATTHEW Ch 6 v 34
So do not worry about tomorrow; it will have enough worries of its own. There is no need to add to the troubles each day brings.

ECCLESIASTES Ch 3 v 1-2
Everything that happens in this world happens at the time God chooses. He sets the time for birth and the time for death, the time for planting and the time for pulling up, the time for killing and the time for healing, the time for tearing down and the time for building, . . . the time for sorrow and the time for joy, the time for mourning and the time for dancing, the time for making love and the time for not making love, the time for kissing and the time for not kissing. He sets the time for finding and the time for losing. . . . for saving and for throwing away, . . . for tearing and mending, . . . for silence and talk. He sets the time for love and for hate, . . . for war . . . and peace.

FURTHER READINGS

Isaiah Ch 12 v 4-6   Daniel Ch 2 v 20-21   Psalm 37 v 7
                    Psalm 90 v 4

THOUGHT

If we take great care of the minutes, then surely the hours will take care of themselves. The value of our life will not be taken by the duration, but by the donation - what we have put into it. Right now the time we have - we must use wisely.

PRAYER

We can but thank you Lord God, for the three score years and ten that you do give to each of us. Keep us mindful of the unknown return date that you have already planned and help our every waking hour to be spent either in work, rest or play, but befitting your ever watchful presence.

SO LET IT BE

♪ **I NEED THEE EVERY HOUR** ♪

TRUTH

2 TIMOTHY Ch 3 v 16
All scripture is inspired by God and is useful for teaching the truth, rebuking errors, correcting faults, and giving instruction for right living.

JOHN Ch 18 v 37
. . . Jesus answered, "You say that I am King. I was born and came into this world for this one purpose, to speak about the truth. Whoever belongs to the truth, listens to me."

PROVERBS Ch 12 v 19
A lie has a short life, but truth lives forever.

JOHN Ch 8 v 31-32
Jesus said to those who believed in him, "If you obey my teaching, you are really my disciples; you will know the truth, and the truth will set you free."

FURTHER READINGS
John Ch 14 v 6 *John Ch 16 v 13* *Psalm 25 v 5*
1 Corinthians Ch 5 v 10

THOUGHT
At each life end all will be revealed and that which is covered up now will become uncovered and every truth will be known. For the repentant Christian there is nothing to fear, everything to gain.

PRAYER
Lead me Lord, into the path of your choosing and show me the passage of truth at all times, no matter how difficult this may prove or how uncertain I might feel. Make me a person of honest ways, as a witness to others of your truths.

SO LET IT BE

Bodmin Moor

♪BREATHE ON ME BREATH OF GOD♫

WISDOM

JAMES Ch 1 v 5
But if any of you lacks wisdom, he should pray to God, who will give it to him because God gives generously and graciously to all.

ECCLESIASTES Ch 8 v 1
Only a wise man knows what things really mean. Wisdom makes him smile and his frowns disappear.

PROVERBS Ch 2 v 6
It is the Lord who gives wisdom; from him comes knowledge and understanding. He provides help and protection for the righteous, honest man. He protects those who treat others fairly, and guards those who are devoted to him.

PROVERBS Ch 8 v 11-12
"I am wisdom, I am better than jewels. Nothing you want can compare with me. I am wisdom, I am insight; I have knowledge and sound judgement."

FURTHER READINGS
Proverbs Ch 14 v 33   Proverbs Ch 3 v 17-18   Ecclesiastes Ch 7 v 19-20
James Ch 3 v 17-18   Job Ch 11 v 12

THOUGHT
If we do not think successfully and do not act wisely, then all the wisdom we may have obtained counts for nought. If we listen to advice and are willing to learn, then we will without doubt become wise. The greatest strength of life is wisdom.

PRAYER
Lord God, help me to understand all that you would say to me. Give me the desire to find wisdom in all that I do and to live according to your teaching. May this wisdom you give to me reflect itself in all my dealings with other people.

SO LET IT BE

♪ COME DOWN O LOVE DIVINE ♫

WORK

ROMANS Ch 12 v 11
Work hard and do not be lazy. Serve the Lord with a heart full of devotion.

PROVERBS Ch 10 v 22
It is the Lord's blessing that makes you wealthy. Hard work can make you no richer.

EPHESIANS Ch 6 v 7-8
Do your work as slaves cheerfully, as though you served the Lord, and not merely men. Remember that the Lord will reward everyone, whether slave or free, for the good work he does.

PROVERBS Ch 21 v 25-26
A lazy man who refuses to work is only killing himself; all he does is think about what he would like to have. A righteous man, however, can give, and give generously.

FURTHER READINGS

2 Thessalonians Ch 7 v 10b   1 Corinthians Ch 15 v 58   Proverbs Ch 12 v 9
Proverbs Ch 14 v 22-23

THOUGHT

It's not "if only" but it is actually doing the very best we can with opportunities which are at hand and wherever we already are. From there, progress will come as and when God wishes it to be so. The devil triumphs when good men do nothing worthwhile.

PRAYER

O God in heaven, give to me a continuing supply of work. Give to me also an ability to find or recreate more work when one task completes. There is so much unfinished work here on earth, especially in the perfecting of your world on loan to mankind, which includes me.

SO LET IT BE

Cheddar Gorge

♪ BLESS THE LORD O MY SOUL, ♫
AND ALL THAT IS IN ME

HELP LINES

CHRISTIAN ENQUIRY AGENCY   0171 620 0718
Welcomes ALL enquiries on the Christian faith

CATHOLIC ENQUIRY CENTRE   0181 455 9871
Welcomes enquiries on the Catholic faith

JEWS FOR JESUS   0171 431 9636
For free Newsletter and all relevant enquiries

METHODIST ENQUIRY SERVICE   0171 222 8010
Welcomes enquiries on the Christian faith

S.O.S. PRAYERLINE 8.00pm-1.00am   01243 371766
Prayer help for anyone in any kind of need

CROSSLINE - CHRISTIAN   0131 555 3333
Listening helpline and prayer support

QUAKER HOME SERVICE   0171 387 3601
Welcomes enquiries on Quaker faith and practice

**A WARM WELCOME AND NEW FRIENDSHIPS
WITHIN YOUR LOCAL CHURCH**

Surprise!

said Jesus to his friends 3 days after they buried him . . .

Would you like to know more about this Christian faith?
WRITE FREEPOST
And you will receive a free information pack.
No one will contact you further unless you ask.
Christian Enquiry Agency
FREEPOST, London, SE1 7YX

Delighted!

to hear from you if this book has been of help. . .

Can you likewise help another with their own copy? See your retailer or
WRITE FREEPOST
And you will receive a post paid order form.
The book together with matching envelope makes a lasting gift.
GRE Publisher
FREEPOST, Essex, IG9 5BR

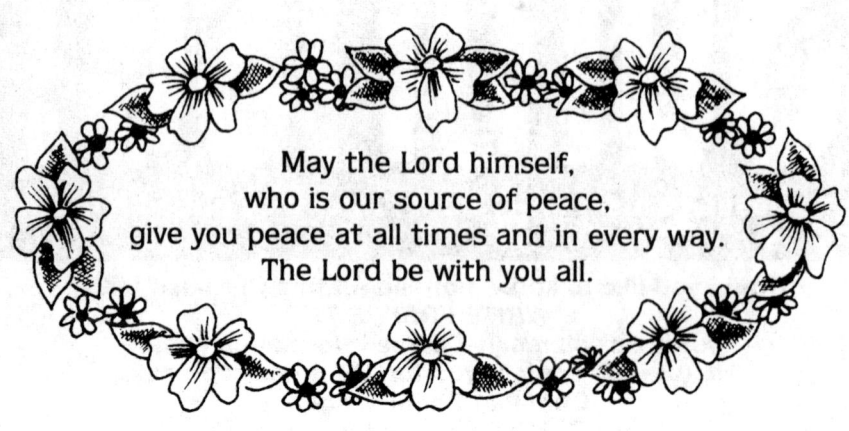

May the Lord himself,
who is our source of peace,
give you peace at all times and in every way.
The Lord be with you all.

These words in a second letter from the Apostle Paul, to his friends the people of Thessalonica - Greece.
And frequently used as a Christian blessing today.

every different kind.

Then God made a man and woman.

that would be called an ark.

Noah took his family into the ark

and two of every animal and bird.

And it rained

It rained for forty days and nights

till the water was everywhere.

Finally it stopped.

The ark landed on a mountaintop.

Noah sent out a dove, and it came back with a leafy branch.

So the earth was getting dry.

Finally, all the animals and Noah left the ark.

And Noah thanked God for saving them.

God put a rainbow in the sky

And said there would never be another flood like this one.

You can read about Noah and the ark in Genesis 6:5-9:17.

Joseph and His Coat

This is Joseph with his new coat.

It's a beautiful coat.

Joseph's brothers were jealous.